MYTHOS

Song of the Siren

FALL 2020

Thank You

ELENA PEREZ
VALERIE KEMP

*Song of the
Siren*

MYTHOS
mythosmagazine.com | @mythos.mag

EDITOR IN CHIEF
JORDAN NISHKIAN | wordsbyjordan.com

EDITORIAL ASSISTANT
REBECCA CARLYLE | @beckscarlyle

PUBLISHED BY
INK AND QUILL PUBLICATIONS

Featuring

AARON WAGONER | aaronwagoner.com @aaron.woah
ALLISON EGUCHI | @allisoneguchi
AUDREY KEMP | audreykempphoto.com
BRITTANY LAWRENCE | theblaw.com @the.b.law
CASSIE NEGUS | @bubblescass
DEANNA NGUYEN | deefordaydreams.com @deefordaydreams
ETHAN A. BAKER
GILES STUART
HJ MORALES
HOLLY KING | hollyisking.com
IAN MCGINNIS | @ianmcg60
JANICE PEREGRINA
JOSEPH NICOLAS DUARTE
josephnduarte1023.myportfolio.com @ojoanonimos
KSENIA PRO | @kseniaprophoto
LIZ MICHAUD | lizmichaud.com
MATTHEW MELENDREZ | @casadelacarniceria
MEGAN HOLDER | @lilmegz_
NATE BUSSEY
NICOLE MILLER | @beautybynicolebreanne
RACHEL LEANNE DELAURENTI
TABITHA LAWRENCE
TAMARA LINDSEY | @scribingsparrow
TAYLOR WISE
TONY NGUYEN | @tonynguyentattoos

FALL 2020 | ISSUE 1

Contents

CONTENTS

Stories

Photography

THE SILENT SIREN

WRITTEN BY JANICE PEREGRINA

peer in, look through the porthole
at the ocean, vast as sin
the silent siren rises
from the black within

the water's growing colder
her white hate arrests your breath
mouth agape, now screaming
screams a summons for your death

a million miles down below
beyond where men have tread
the siren takes another
who dared disrupt her bed

LAST EMBRACE

by MATTHEW MELENDREZ

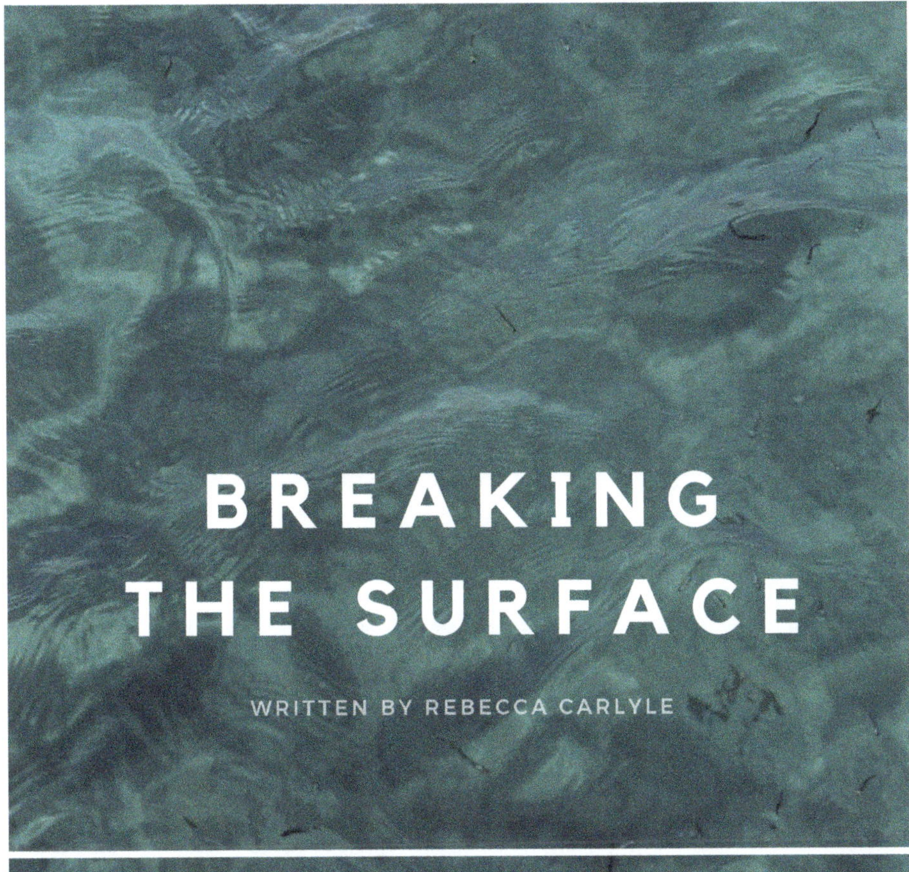

BREAKING THE SURFACE

WRITTEN BY REBECCA CARLYLE

The fire crackled and hissed at her from across the room, the orange light flickering upon the stone walls. She arrived late in the evening a week ago; it was too dark to take in her surroundings. A friend of hers had asked her to look after their cousin's cabin for two weeks, and she jumped at the opportunity to get out of town—a break from the hustle and bustle of city life was much needed.

Unsure of what to pack for her extended stay away from home, she stuffed her duffle bag with everything she thought she could possibly need. Warm clothes to cool clothes, sunscreen and bug spray, toothpaste and shampoo, she wanted to be prepared for anything. She nabbed a shower towel and a pillow from the house, raided the PopTarts and some chips from the pantry, and loaded her bags into the trunk of her Silk Blue Metallic Jetta before setting off on her journey.

The drive lasted three hours into the mountains, weaving her through the pine trees and down roads she never knew existed. She rolled down the window to enjoy the fresh air. Although she had never been up this way herself, she did recognize a few pull-over spots from her friend's Facebook. About a third of the way through there was the mom-and-pop BBQ house they always stopped at for lunch, and about an hour after that was the Starbucks they always used for bathroom breaks.

About two hours into the drive, she lost all cell reception, forcing her to pull over and retrieve a paper map from the glove compartment, a gift from her chronically over-prepared parents. She thought her parents silly when they had given it to her, thinking she would never need it. The city was a grid, and the only place you would lose cell service is the underground parking garages. Her mother's face popped into her mind as she unfolded the crisp paper and tried to figure out which way she was supposed to hold it. It took her awhile to find where she was currently parked among the tangles of so many different colored lines.

Once she found where she was on the map it was pretty simple to figure out where to turn off and which long, winding driveway to take. However, she didn't turn her music back up and she frequently checked where she was in relation to where she needed to go. The last few roads had no streetlights on them and she had to drive with her cab light on in order to read the map that she held flush to the steering wheel. When she arrived at the single story—possibly one room—wood paneled cabin, the brass key was exactly where she was told it would be: under a loose stone from the peony-lined walkway.

The first night was cold, and she didn't know where anything was in the dark. Of course the one thing she forgot to pack in her bags was a flashlight. She thought of using the flashlight app on her phone, but she had killed the battery letting her phone search for service. She fumbled through the rooms, letting her hands run along the walls, feeling for the switches that never announced their presence to her fingers. She finally found the bed, collapsing on top of the blankets, wafts of dust drifting around her and letting herself succumb to sleep.

From the depths of her slumber, her mind felt weighted down, burdened with all the stress she had been feeling lately. She swam through them, pricking each stress bubble with a needle and listening to them as they hissed, losing pressure. She began floating, as if the air she released had filled her up like a balloon. Weightless and relaxed, she felt the tension leave her and let the ebbing of her mind swirl her around.

The next morning, she woke refreshed and decided to start by exploring the four-room cabin: bedroom, bathroom, kitchen, and living room. It was small, with barely the basics stocked. The fireplace had a stack of logs ready to light—one or two would easily warm the small space. The kitchen window looked out into the backyard which butted against an incredibly blue lake. Throughout the day she found herself drawn to the window, gazing at it. It reminded her of a sapphire as it sparkled in the light of the clear sun. Her grandmother always had sea glass hanging in the windows and they glinted when the sun hit them just right.

Looking about herself, she wondered when was the last time that the cabin had housed anyone. She decided to get a fire going so that she wouldn't have to learn how to do so after the heat of the day had disappeared. It took awhile as she had to hunt down the matches first. They were hidden in a kitchen drawer. Feeling the heat on her fingertips when striking the matches made her flinch. She understood she wasn't going to spontaneously catch fire, but the irrational fear remained causing her heart to leap when she struck a match. She grew up with a gas fireplace and had never needed to start an actual fire, besides using a lighter to start the pilot.

A seemingly long time later, a small flame finally caught and she carefully placed the screen back in front of the fireplace. She expected it to roar into life like it did in the movies, but merely crackled quietly.

Consistently for four nights she awoke before the sun to find that she was absolutely frigid. At first she tried to sleep through it, merely rolling over and burrowing her face in her pillow from home. She learned to prep herself by wearing sweats, a thermal shirt, and two layers of socks to bed. Even so, she awoke shivering. On the fifth night, she crept out into the kitchen to make herself some scaldingly hot tea and perched herself by the fireplace. Although the flames were gone, it still put off some warmth. She eventually fell asleep on the hearth, waking the next morning with stiff muscles. She had originally decided not to dig through too many of their personal belongings, feeling uncomfortable with going through their effects. However, her chilled skin and achy neck persuaded her it was necessary to go through the closets looking for extra blankets. She found a thick wool blanket in the back of the bedroom closet, behind musty winter coats and placed it on the foot of the bed.

She opened the front door and took a step outside. She had been wanting to go exploring through the surrounding forest, but had worried she would get lost. The day before she had lost an unknown amount of time looking out the window, trying to track the pathway from the house to the lake. Maybe today was the day. The crisp morning air wrapped around her small frame, making her very aware of how thin her yoga leggings were and how loosely-knit her sweater was. She immediately retreated inside.

Instead, she meandered into the kitchen and toasted a PopTart. The strawberry jam that oozed between her teeth was a simple pleasure that paired perfectly with sitting at the kitchen window, staring longingly at the water. Her mind wandered, imagining fins slicing through the water playfully spraying the mermaid perched on the dock.

After rinsing the crumbs and a smudge of jam off of her plate, she wandered between the three main rooms aimlessly, looking for anything to do. She walked in

circles, her eyes wandering, searching for something to
hone in on. The bookcase in the living room was
crammed full of cheap pulp mysteries. She could read
a book she supposed. She always read the reviews for
books in magazines and online articles and would buy
them, but never had time to actually read them. She
brought a few of them with her with the hopes that she
would finally read them, but she wasn't so sure that
was how she wanted to spend her time. Instead, she
opted to read the back flaps of the books displayed on
the dusty, pinewood case across from the window. As
she tipped the books off of their shelves, she wondered
if the books had ever been read—some of the bindings
were smooth and the pages were unwrinkled.

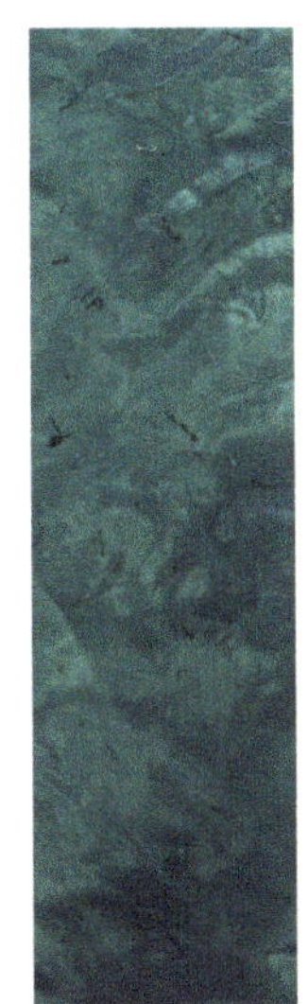

That night, she found herself going to bed fairly early, not because she
was tired, but because she didn't know what else to do. Her muscles
were sore from sitting on the stone floor, slouching over piles of books.
As she stood, she tried to brush the floor indents out of her skin. The
sun was barely down, but the twin sized bed called her name. Luckily
the blanket she had found in the closet earlier was warmer than the
old, worn-out quilt she had covering her the night before. She awoke
some time later. The silence of the woods was surprisingly loud.
Rustling branches, crickets, twigs snapping—all things that put her on
edge. She sat up, pulling the sheets and blankets around her
shoulders before rising from the creaky mattress. Her socks padded
the sound of her feet sliding across the floors throughout the cabin.

Wrapped in blankets, she found herself standing by the window in the
kitchen, not quite sure how she had gotten there. The fire had died
down, but the embers still cast a glow throughout the room, lending
just enough light for her to see. The lake was luminous in the
moonlight—serene and picturesque. The water rippled as if something
had disturbed the surface. She thought maybe a fallen leaf or a fish
from below, but couldn't help noticing that the rippling moved in
time with her breathing. It was like a meditation, watching the water
sway back and forth and forth and back. She wasn't sure if her
reflection in the window was just her sleepy mind making everything
appear cloudy, and the air seem stale and the walls stifling.

She didn't remember leaving the kitchen, but by the time her mind had refocused on her surroundings, she was pushing the cabin door open. The blankets and sheets fell from her shoulders, leaving a trail behind her. The wet of dew covered leaves and ground barely perturbed her as she passed by. She pushed branches to the side as she moved through the forest.

She emerged onto the edge of the lake, her body still despite the surrounding cold. The breeze kissed the top of the still water, setting the lake into iridescent waves before her. She felt the impulse to throw herself into the depths, to feel the cool water seep into her skin and fill her with its serenity.

The water beckoned to her, calling her name, with the early morning mist echoing it back. She moved forward onto the short dock, the chipped wood planks almost startling her out of her reverie; but the swaying of the dock beneath her bare feet moved with the rhythm that pulsed in her veins. The wind pulled at her clothes, ushering her even closer to the end and pulling her feet off the edge of the dock. She was weightless for a moment before plunging feet-first into cold silence.

The air pummeled from her lungs, escaping in large bubbles about her face. Still, she continued to descend further, deeper, her eyelids refusing to open. Her body felt frantic without air, craving it. Her cotton pajama pants and thermal top were heavy and weighed her down, making it difficult to move her legs through the water. She was torn. Despite her body begging for the surface, something told her to go deeper, pulling her to the bottom of the lake.

This was real silence, unlike the city where it was always buzzing outside and unlike the woods where there was always buzzing in her mind. Everything was quiet, muted, soft. The lake water caressed her skin and sunk into her pores. She let the lake push her body around, swaying in a way that felt like an up and down motion, even though she was sinking.

She continued to descend until her feet hit the bottom, her soles settling among the lakeweeds onto smooth, algal rocks. Her eyes opened—everything was dark. Although the moon created some light to see by up above, here beneath the water was nothing. Her lungs burned but she didn't push off the ground. She felt her toes take root around the rocks, anchoring her there. Her hair flowed all about her, and her weightless arms floated in front of her. The pressure in her lungs faded and she closed her eyes once more, her heartbeat slowing to pulse in time with the swaying, silent lake.

Lament

WRITTEN BY DEANNA NGUYEN

Winds of a moon-soaked night,
carry her voice
as gentle as the caresses
of a mother cradling
her newborn child.

Rising and falling
like the ocean waves,
her song tickles the ears
of those who are lost
in a familiar loneliness.

Never dissipating,
the mystic lyrics
seep into the chasms
of a memory yet known
but always present.

She shares a world
so secret, so elusive
that searching for it
dissolves the edges
of a waking dream.

Her story
shall echo and resonate
across unreached waters,
to the one destined
to end with her.

IN FLIGHT
photographed by
KSENIA PRO
model: ALLISON EGUCHI

WRITTEN BY JORDAN NISHKIAN
PHOTOGRAPHED BY IAN MCGINNIS

You once heard that you could
figure out which way was up
by following the bubbles.

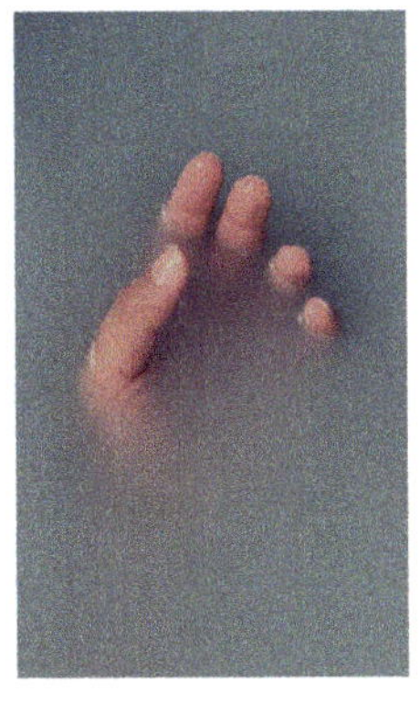

You weren't sure when it had started, but the tinnitus that haunted your right ear had now wrapped around your head and entered your left. At first, it was something you only heard in silence—now there were days when the ringing was nearly debilitating.

You pushed through work until the new guy with the compass tattoo relieved your shift in the parking lot attendant booth. Summer was over; even at four, the sky left you wanting for daylight.

The thirty-minute walk home was littered with crescendos of ringing in your ears—aggravated by squealing tires and blasts of bass-heavy music—but it quieted down by the time your heavy feet trudged up the stairs to your studio apartment.

Though it had been two months since Mara moved out, you were half expecting to hear the chatter from one of her shows when you opened your door. You didn't miss her need for noise, but you did miss the bread she learned to bake by watching British people compete for a cake stand, the superstitious habits she developed when she watched something too scary, the lack of space she left on your walls. You missed how she could sing along to any song.

You never noticed the ringing until she left—maybe there was something to her strategy.

Eight hours in the attendant booth left you with a film of stale exhaust settling into your skin. The patter of water in the shower was usually the only type of ambient distraction that could appease the ringing, but perhaps it was the steam.

You reached your arm behind the clear plastic shower curtain and turned the water-spotted knob. A rattle in the pipes released a sluggish trickle from the showerhead. After weeks of warning, the shower arm had finally given out on you.

You tried your luck with the tub faucet, smacking down the calcified peg that directed water to your now-useless showerhead. Tepid water flowed out of the teal-tinged tap, and once it warmed up a bit, you pressed down on the drain stopper until you felt it click into place.

The water crashing into the acrylic tub became a part of the city soundtrack as you walked across the apartment to the kitchen. You dried your hand on a rumpled up towel on the counter and glanced over your uninspired pantry, opting to pour yourself half a mug of the black spiced rum Mara left behind.

The ringing swelled, but before your hand could reach your ear, it quieted. It was still there, but not as sharp, like the reverberation after striking a bell. You swallowed the contents of your novelty mug without setting it down, flooding your throat with a slow-draining burn that was quick to seep into your lungs and your stomach.

The rum did nothing for the humming, but it helped your memory.

You set the empty mug on the counter and made your way back to the tub, stepping out of your scuffed sneakers and taking off your navy-polo-and-black-pants uniform. You left your clothes in a pile by your bed, noticing that the hum was getting louder by the time your bare feet felt the linoleum.

You pulled the curtain aside and turned off the tap, testing the temperature with your hand before stepping into the overfilled tub. Easing your body into the water caused it to slosh over the edge and onto the floor, instantly soaking the dollar-store bath mat beside it.

The warmth of the water was forgiving and lent you a feeling of lightness that you hadn't felt in years. Small waves rocked you, and you began finding rhythms in the hum. Eyes closed, you tilted your head back until your ears filled with bathwater. You expected the sound to be muffled and cloudy, but it only became clearer and more familiar.

Your fingers curled around the edge of the tub as you pulled yourself up from under the surface. Your eyes darted around the bathroom—you were alone and her humming had softened. Easing your spine against the wall of the tub, you let your eyes close again, trying to block out the sound with the gentle lapping of warm water against the walls of the tub. The steam rose and collected around your nose and across your brow. Despite your best efforts, her melody lingered in your mind and beckoned you to listen.

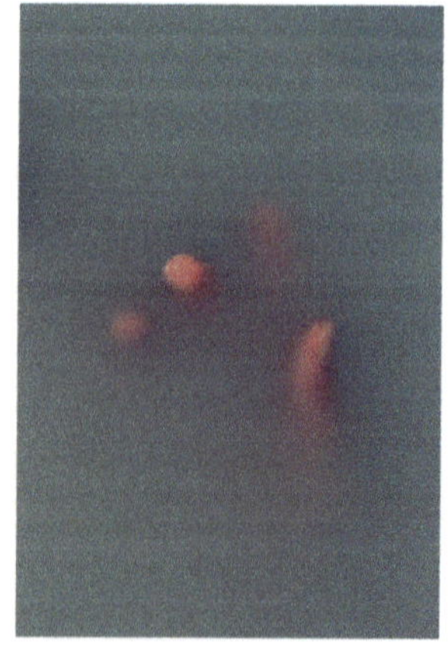

Lungs filled, you prepared to submerge yourself. You lowered your face into the water, greeted by the sound of her voice. Your body sunk into the weightlessness as you opened your eyes, looking for the source of the song. Soft yellow light poured in from your ceiling, and there was nothing to see besides your own blurred limbs.

Your lids lowered closed as you began moving your arms to the tune of her voice. The places where your vertebrae anchored you to the floor of the tub detached until each part of you was swaddled in water.

Legs outstretched, you started to kick, feeling self-initiated currents pummel between your toes. The darkness behind your eyelids embedded you in the rise and fall of her otherworldly pitch and the push and pull of the water, which had grown colder.

You arched your back and paddled your limbs in circles. Small whirlpools churned behind your knees and shoulders. You felt a freedom in expanding, in feeling your muscles stretch out in a glorious yawn after being confined to the limitations of concurrent compartmentalization.

Her song became louder, and you felt a neighboring current swirl around you. You swore her fingers were interlacing yours, that her hair was painting waves over your shoulders and chest.

You opened your eyes, and in the split second you could bare the burn of salt, you saw you were swallowed in openness—still alone, feeling your lungs pinch and contract with deprivation. You clawed for the walls of the tub, but all you could sense was a cold and briny expanse. Forcing your eyes open, you found yourself lost in indigo—a directionless space with no division of light and dark.

You once heard that you could figure out which way was up by following the bubbles.

Ready to kick, you unsealed your lungs, hoping your last small ration of air could lead you to the surface.

Tides sway washing sand waltz
grandma's hands scrape soapy ribbed metal.
Foam brews, grunts splash in the air
salting lungs, cleaning carbon.

She drained dirty water on grass,
Simba, the dog, rolled on mud to cool.
Eres un puerco, the Boxer's flat, perfect snout.
No tienes verguenza, shameless he slept in cool filth.

Summer burned through, desert's sun boiled
mercury as we drove to the Gulf's timid shore.
She lay her towel on the grey sand beach
sprinkled with beer cans and coals.

She looked at the sky pleading, her skin
salted by air. *Porque estas enojado?*
Sizzling, she walked into foam
her knees folded as water grasped her neck.

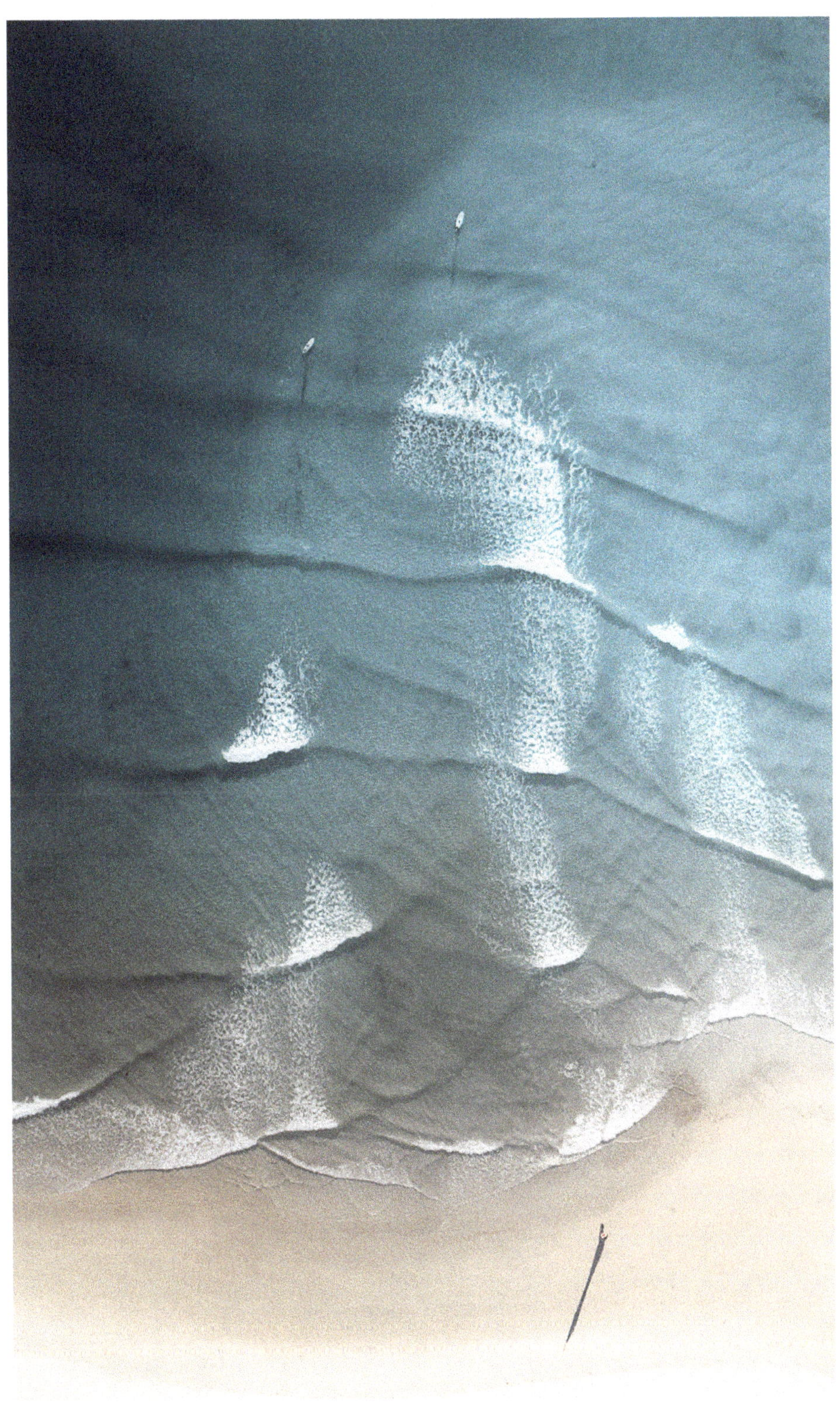

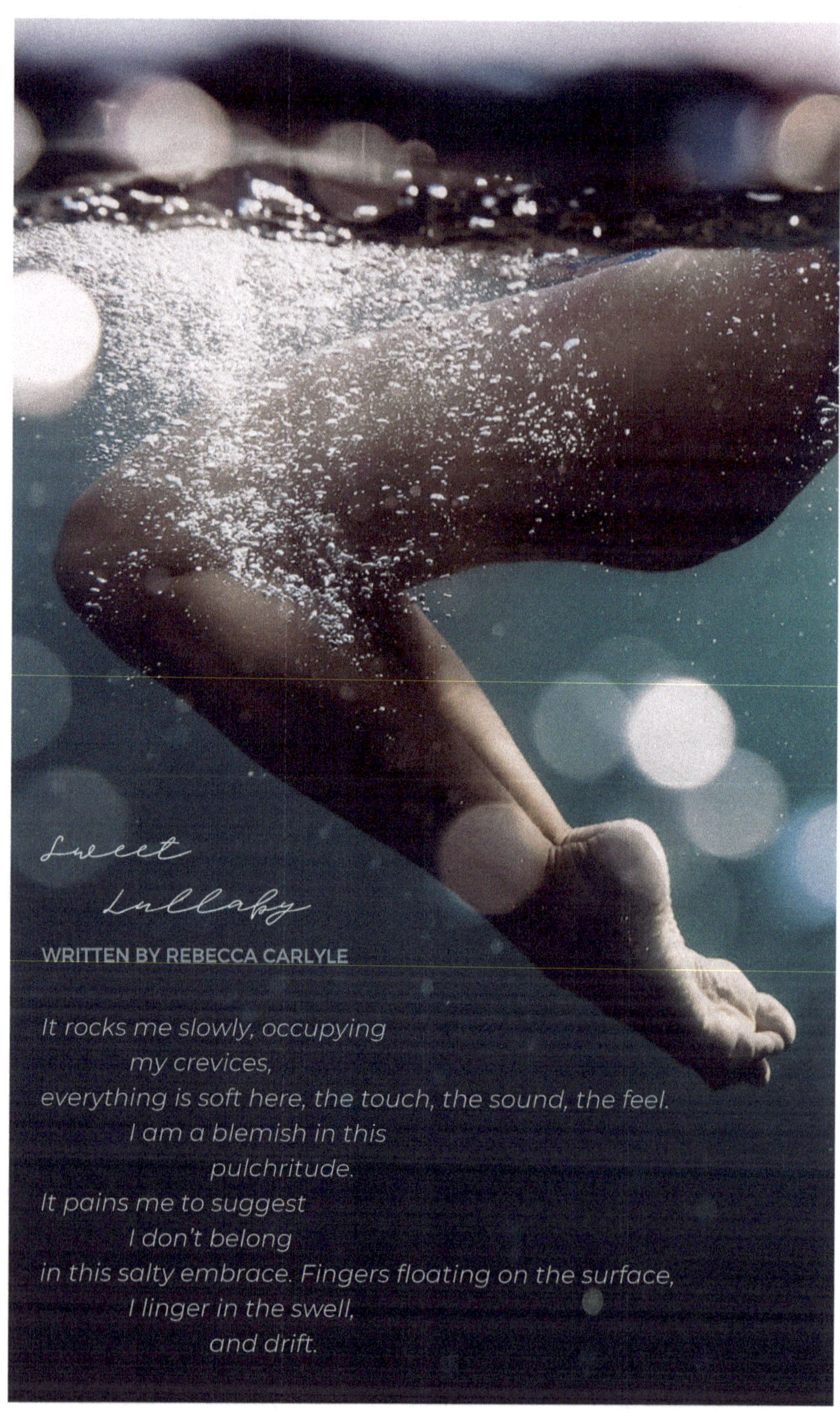

Sweet
Lullaby

WRITTEN BY REBECCA CARLYLE

It rocks me slowly, occupying
        my crevices,
everything is soft here, the touch, the sound, the feel.
        I am a blemish in this
                pulchritude.
It pains me to suggest
        I don't belong
in this salty embrace. Fingers floating on the surface,
        I linger in the swell,
                and drift.

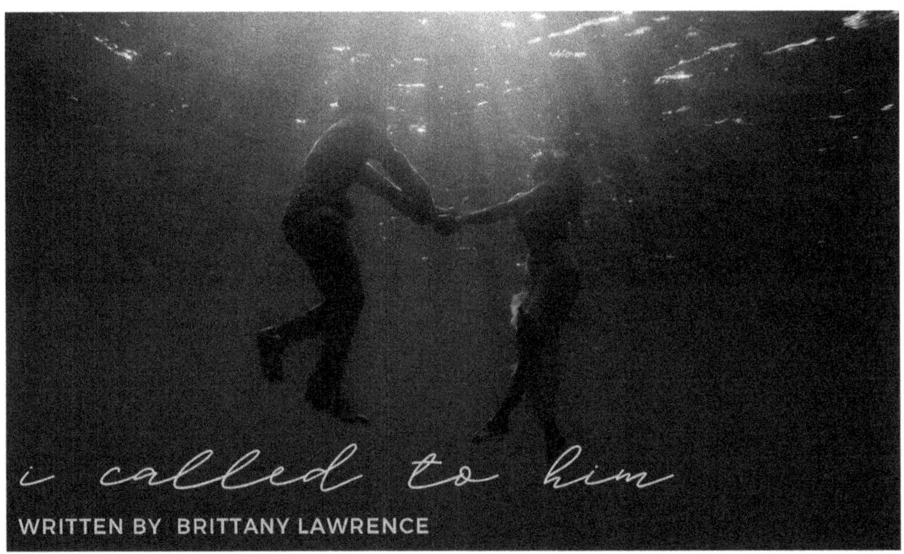

His siren call was elsewhere, leaving the wreckage behind. Me, broken on the floor with all of my pieces. Left in the middle of a shipwreck, he took my treasure and was gone. I watched as the parts of me he didn't want lost their last hints of shimmer as the sun set, and then there was just darkness.

He called to me, with a look filled of fire and alcohol, igniting my senses with false clarity. I no longer felt the storm of the past upon me, just the certainty that going forward would get me through the night. Each playful nudge and subtle graze was like the fog rolling in, setting the scene for mystery and adventure. He called me again, and this time I met his fiery gaze, following him into the fog. As my eyes adjusted, I was jolted back to the hard reality. Chaos. Sharp rocks lining tall cliffs. Swells overtaking the bow, and drowning me in every meant to be thought. Little fool. And you, sitting upon your rock, looking down at the mess you created. A storm that you put into motion. A masterpiece of perfectly misplaced parts that could never get too close. As I passed by, you didn't even notice me. You were too busy casting your siren song, luring the next non-suspecting girl into the depths of the fog. But I would not go down with this ship and be washed away with the tide. If a song was what got me here, then I would learn to sing.

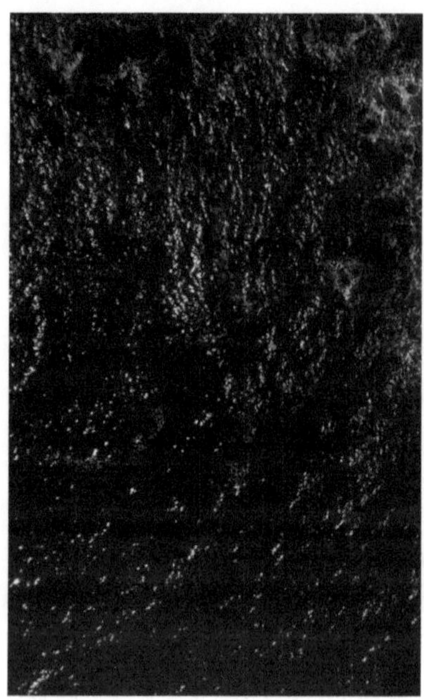

The sun reflected off my glistening skin, letting me soak up its power. I'd been dancing on this beach for months. There were no sailors there. Just a few maidens with scars and tales of pirates. Fireside stories that almost felt like make believe when told with the right amount of intoxicated allure. It was peaceful, but deep down something was stirring. Far off, the horizon looked fuzzy. The winds were blowing something in, and although we knew not what, a sense of excited anticipation overcame us. But it's not just we who felt it. It was almost as if everything on the beach had absorbed its energy. All was electric and awake, too full of life to even dull when the night came. Life glowed on the beach, illuminated by the moon like it was a spotlight just for us. Or maybe we were too blind to see that the the spotlight wasn't shining for us at all. Far out on the fuzzy horizon, as if out of thin air, sails were coming in with the tide. My toes suddenly burned in the cool sand, and before I could even stop myself, I called to them with a rum filled song. A sound so sweet, I almost believed it myself.

He was gorgeous. Our eyes locked and the roar of the waves turned into a beating hum, hypnotizing anyone who would listen. I tried to keep my song going, but the hum was so strong I could feel it reverberating through my bones. I could not help but give in to him. And so he swept me up, drunk and sure, and led me towards his ship. I had never seen anything more grand. Tall rooms that glittered and a view of the horizon I had never experienced. My beach getting smaller in the distance, glowing under the moon. You whispered your sweet song in my ear and I was yours. The waters were calm and the stars were sparkling so bright that I didn't even notice your eyes had gone dark as you closed the doors.

As quickly as you wanted me, you were done with me.

The calm waters were suddenly surging and havoc broke out over the deck. I stood on the plank, high above the black water, and in the distance I could see my little beach, now glowing with fire as it turned into ash. My safe paradise where I should have stayed. I turned to look at you one more time, but you already had your back to me like I wasn't even there, so I stepped off. The water, dark and cold, received me with open arms. When I came to the surface you were gone, like a ghost ship that was only just a myth. I closed my eyes and let the current take me to wherever I would land, feeling its power. The waves bobbed up and down, but were gentle with me. Through the sound of the water, I could hear it telling me I was not done yet.

I saw them. The ones always chosen, but who never choose for long. Leaving a trail of broken hearts in their wakes, like chum in the water.

Good hearts left to believe they were only good enough for sharks,

ripping them apart as so many before had done. I saw their eyes, searching for their next kills, ships underway with a fierce wind in their sails.

I laid atop my rock, watching from a distance as both vessels came into view, gaudy and awful. These were not what I last remembered. Once shiny and beautiful now looked cheap and sad. Their magical facades chipped away with every wave. I breathed in the salty air and smiled, knowing they would hardly recognize me, for I had evolved. Their carelessness like fairy dust covered me, and when I arose, strong and beautiful, I knew I could not break. A maniacal energy stirred inside me, waking my senses and all my surroundings. I took my stance upon my rock that I built, tall and magnificent. High enough to protect me from the sharks at sea, but they didn't know this yet. I closed my eyes and felt the breeze on my face, and when I opened them, I saw my prey, and so I called to them.

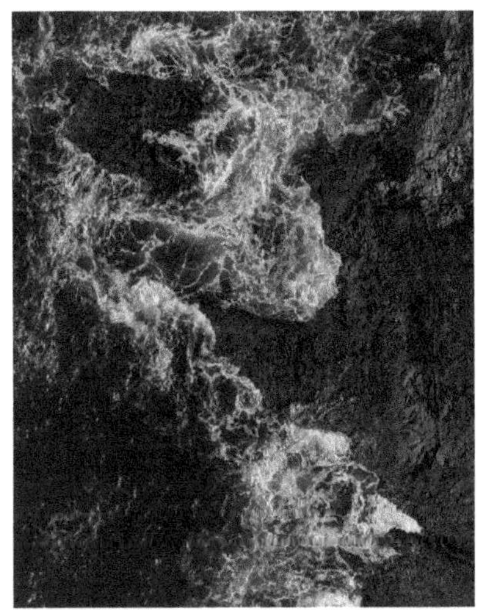

A SIREN'S CRY

WRITTEN BY TAMARA LINDSEY

Lover hear my harmony.
Come find me.
Search the midnight fury.
I'm crying.

Lover hear my harmony.
Unite with me.
Search the midnight fury.
I'm lonely.

Lover hear my harmony.
Don't leave me.
Search the midnight fury.
I'm waiting.

The River God's
Daughters
WRITTEN BY TABITHA LAWRENCE

coarse tangles of hair in clumps and
spirals, soft helmet of frizz, lavender
tinged legs, big Italian snoz. Lots of
sisters and, much later, lots of brothers.
And something else, but I can't put my
finger on it. Sometimes she speaks of
things as though I should know what
she's talking about and I wonder if I do,
somewhere in the tide pools in the
back of my mind.

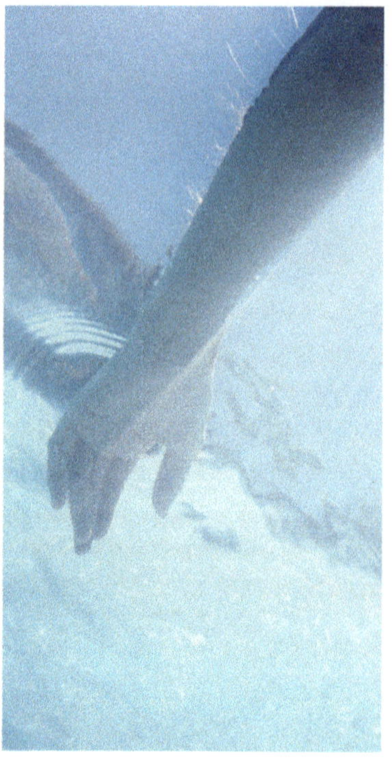

And what was this supposed to be? A
story about a boy who told me about
places, about Dominican folk tales and
rockier coasts, and then disappeared. A
mythical creature just maddening
enough that I have no choice but to be
writing about him still, years later,
when he tries to come back onto the
page. I guess we all have our sirens. But by sirens, of course, I mean
the blind spots we are willing to overlook time and time again. The
dull buzz in our ears after the explosion. My sisters and I watch live
streams of church services from our homes during the pandemic.
The pastor tells us to ask ourselves, how many times will I have to
learn this lesson? We shift in our seats.

And how does this relate? A memory, three girls in the back of a big
white van, the windows painted black (their mother's boyfriend's,
this isn't that kind of story). There's a mattress behind the driver's
seat and the youngest sits on it cross-legged, reading in the glimpse
of streetlights through his window. "What's genitalia?" she sounds
out. Uncle laughs (they're supposed to call him Uncle) and she
reddens, closes the book. "What the hell kind of stuff they got you
reading?"

I don't remember when they stop pretending that the baby is a
tumor, and wow is that sentence something to unpack. I just
remember that by the time the baby arrives, the man we're
supposed to call Uncle is gone. Soon, she is too. You never can
pinpoint when the story she's telling you shifts and inevitably
becomes about him. I'm just thinking of it because I'm thinking of
that happy beach town apartment, one bedroom, bunk beds in the
kitchen, driving in the van singing like a choir, "If I was green, I
would die." I'm thinking of the phone calls we must have missed
when she said answer only if it rings twice, hangs up, and then rings
again.

I don't know how to write fantasy. I don't know how to write anything that didn't sort of happen, and once it's on the page, I don't know how to show people and explain that it's just fiction, only sort of true, don't read into what I had to do to make it into a story. Picture my mother high in her seashell crusted house, painting sunsets and palm trees on the living room wall at 2 AM, my sisters and I in our room, murmuring to each other in our sleep.

The next time, there was almost a wedding. She can't make us call this one Uncle because he's practically our age. For the wedding itself, she has a vision—the Tall Ships Festival, all of us dressed like pirates—still the measure against which we decide if a blouse is too piratey. Would you wear it to Mom's pirate flash mob wedding? If so, put it back on the rack.

Whenever she'd leave, I'd need a full day to recover. I'd be inconsolable. Outwardly, of course, I'd be nothing. I'd get in trouble for an attitude I didn't mean to have. I'd get grounded for sneaking around, making a Myspace to talk to boys whom I knew I could never speak to in person. I wrote on my fictitious profile "My life isn't as perfect as it looks… but it's pretty close" smiley-face heart. I sensed even then that this bereftness was not marketable.

But she gave things magic in her musings. Ordinary things glimmered under her touch. Of course, there were fairies. Of course, there was whole milk, white toast doused in butter.

We all have our sirens—mine is this: I was trying to write about Odysseus. I was trying to write about getting drunk and reading poems about mermaids to a boy, setting into motion years of trying to lay bait in Snapchat stories and equally trivial things, but instead, we got this. What I'm saying is I'm still not sure how to write about you. What I'm saying is I'm always writing about you.

Surely we can pull a story arc out of here, somewhere.

ASANA

BY TONY NGUYEN

DOOM WAIL
WRITTEN BY ETHAN A. BAKER

I am a storm, crammed into a bottle
of forced smiles and recycled
conversations. We all ignore the smoke

from our burning souls as we usher
ourselves into a pit of broken
mirrors. Our hands and feet

bleed as we shuffle our beaten
bones towards the weary
reaper. His list feeds the gluttonous

ground that the sea
wears down with each sigh.
I wish the water could carry me into

the deep where mermaids plant
new tombs. There may I find silence
for a while to swallow the weight
of my bile that drags me into a stupor
of my own stupidity.

Polished marble steps gently
drop me onto the creaking
         quay where ships bob
on the steel blue sea. As turbines

turn, people wave and cheer, watching the ships
         steam towards the promised
land. I wave my ticket, screaming,

         Wait! I have one! Can't you see...

         catching a loose board, my body
launches
into an arc, the side of my face

         ramming the oak
boards, my right knee catching a loose
         nail, my ticket—a wilted piece of paper.

The ships saunter over the shining
horizon with ranks of birds in tow—the Ivory
Tower slips beneath the glass
         water, the wind
dies as the sun
         slumbers. I walk to the end

of the dock to hang my body
over the edge, holding out my ticket
as bait for some wonder

         fish to swallow, or until my muscles
turn to mulch, releasing me into the dark

         descent of sleep where mermaids
throttle the dreams of the walking weary.

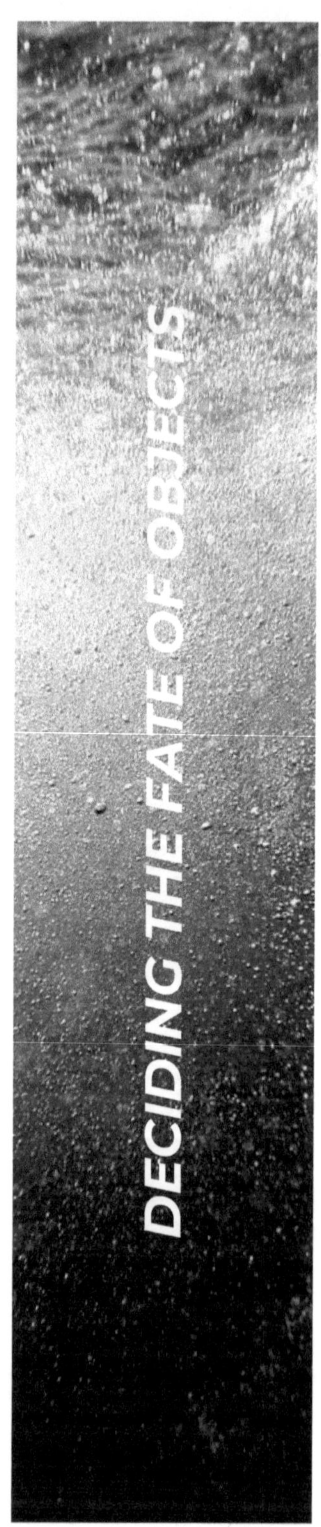

Smoke rushes skyward as black
ash rains across asphalt, helos
vomit water as whining

propeller airplanes dust
hillsides with red crushed
chalk, sirens

echo in-between homes
as bandannas protect
lungs from fluttering
particles—evacuation

sends everyone into turmoil...

What stays and what
goes? Birth certificates, tax
docs, passports—the essentials—what about

grandpa's old bible? What about my library
of worlds—so much time spent in each.

What about the photos
holding the memories of my
life, the out of
tune piano, two dusty
guitars, and the desk I worked so
hard to buy?

Take, take, take, leave...leave, and
take, leave—sadly,
everything else must
burn. No, this cannot

stay. Car jammed with
the pieces of my life's
soul as the rest rests beneath
the falling blade of flame—it must

stay for it is the fate
of these objects to transition
from occupying a space

in my chest to nothing more
than a black scar
upon the earth.

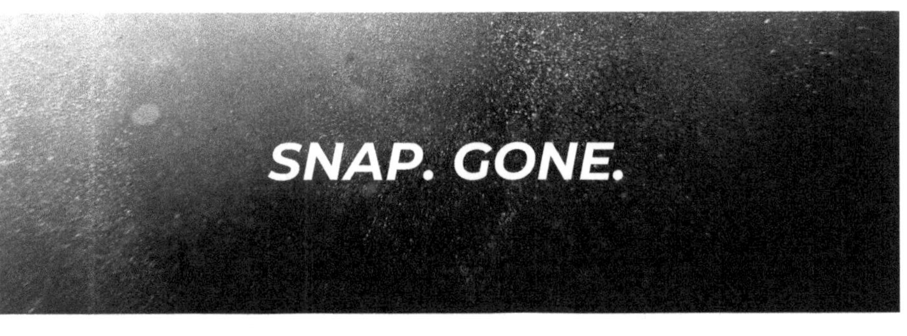

Screeching siren
songs snatch
me out of everyday daydreams
I escape to—

no one is above
Him, he who sleuths
for the next warm
body—it takes a heart

less than a second to stop
beating as metal
crunches into skeleton

coffin. Only after crashing
steel stops do ears
hear the baby's
cries harmonize with

the wailing hollow
wind as it yanks
the autumn
leaves off of Winter's tree—

we brush them
aside, waiting for the next
flood to wash their decaying
corpses out of our concrete
gutters.

I Didn't Want to Kill You

WRITTEN BY RACHEL LEANNE DELAURENTI

I didn't want to do it. I didn't want to kill you.

I'd never experienced that before. Never have I felt guilty for singing, for luring a sailor in, for drowning him. It is, after all, in my nature. Humans are taught from a young age to hunt for food, for sport, for power. For our kind, it is the same.

I didn't want to kill you. When I looked into your deep, golden eyes and placed my hands upon your scruffy, bronzed throat, I felt the depths of Tartarus stir within me. I wanted to keep singing and let you listen to my sweet, siren song.

I didn't want to kill you.

So I killed us both instead.

harp on
WRITTEN, STYLED, AND PHOTOGRAPHED BY AUDREY KEMP
MODEL: TAYLOR WISE

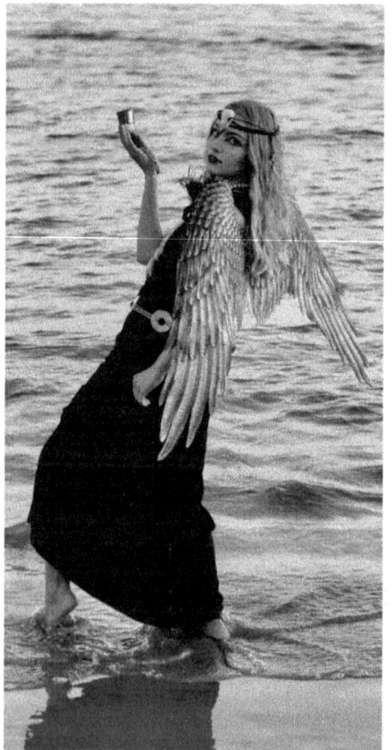

The fate of gorgons is the same:
A woman scorned, easy to blame.
But to discern what sirens seek,
One must look past their plume and beak.

Consider, first, her wailing cry:
Which beckons every passerby --
To navigate the latitude,
And doldrums of her solitude.

Peals of thunder, so beguiling,
She harps on, though seldom smiling;
Her bellows fall on ears nearby,
Yet tragedy is always nigh.

Consider, next, her form, her flesh:
A cursed amalgam, so grotesque --
But female frames are often feared,
And scrutinized, seldom revered.

So sing, O muse, and let her be,
In her domain, the sounding sea.
Harp on, shriek on, and howl and caw;
Her fortitude inspires awe.

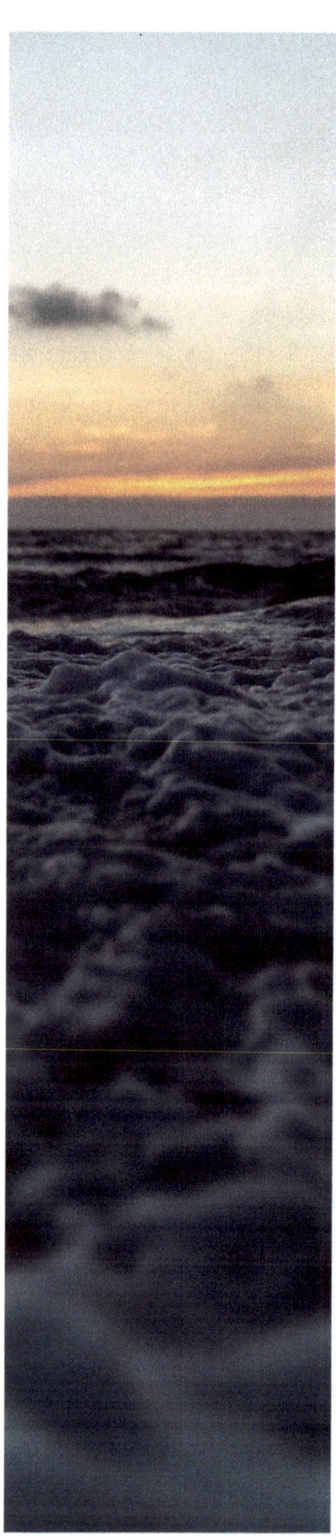

The Other Side of

Paradise

WRITTEN BY HOLLY KING
PHOTOGRAPHY BY AARON WAGONER

The greatest lie she ever told
herself was that her spine
felt burdened from violet
rosebuds pushing out
of each crack in the cement.
That thorns broke open troves
of forgotten dreams.

No whispers could escape
the other side of Paradise.
Not when she planted the seeds
inside her throat, so deep
that even the reaching fingers
of the sun couldn't free
the spark tangled within.

The promise of the siren's litany
said that one day she'd unshackle
chains across her mind. Free the fear
that if she were unleashed upon
this aching world, she'd move waves
with her fingertips, water forests
with each trembling footstep.

If she could unclench her gnashing teeth.
If she could grasp the key unscathed.
If only she dared.

# TAKE CARE

PHOTOGRAPHED BY JOSEPH NICOLAS DUARTE | MODEL: CASSIE NEGUS

A REMINDER TO PROTECT OUR OCEANS AND
THE CREATURES THAT INHABIT THEM

PACIFIC MARINE MAMMAL CENTER
Laguna Beach, CA | pacificmmc.org/ways-to-give

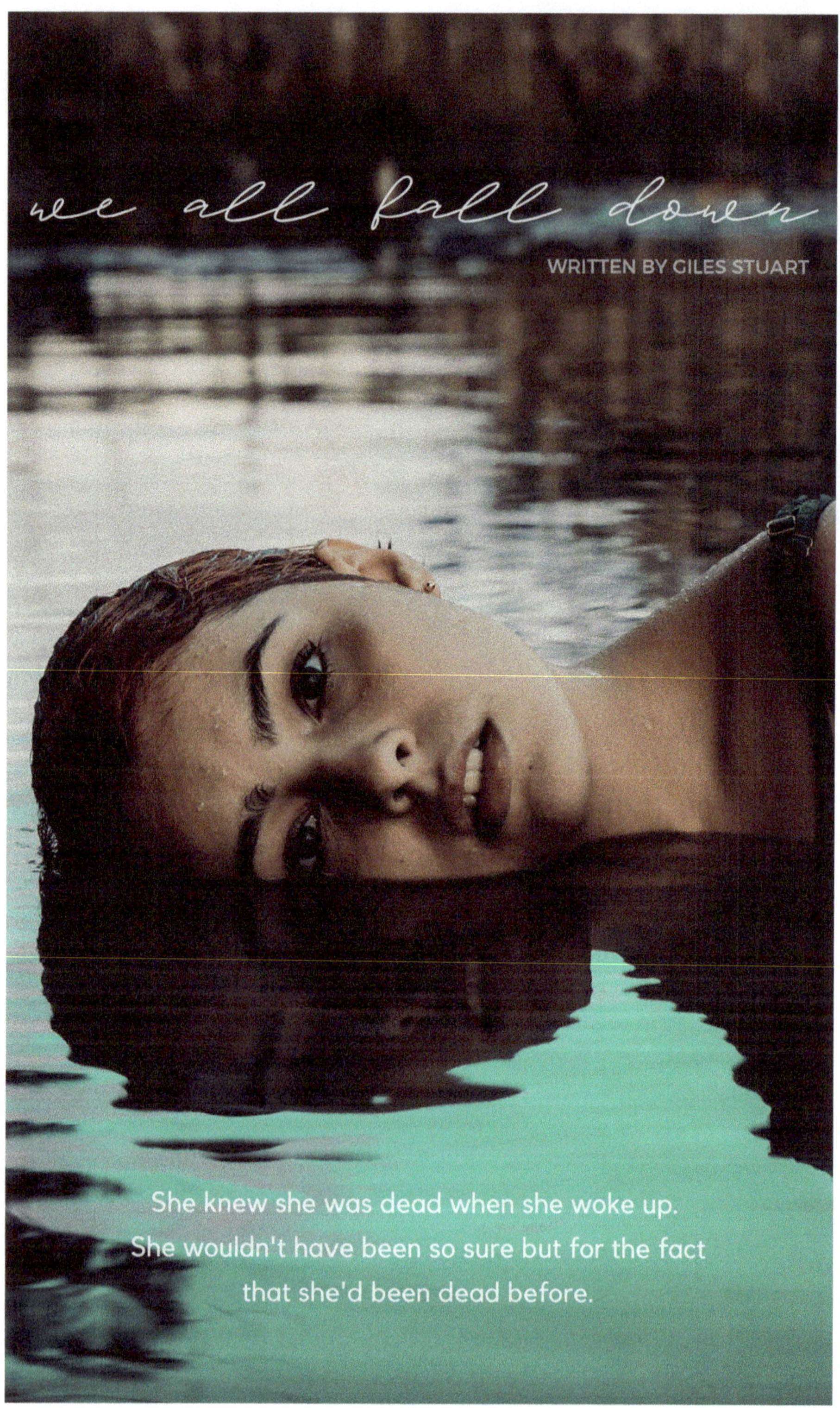

we all fall down
WRITTEN BY GILES STUART
She knew she was dead when she woke up.
She wouldn't have been so sure but for the fact
that she'd been dead before.

A minor surgery had turned into a twenty-four hour nightmare when a routine appendectomy revealed a latent heart condition. Only five, she barely remembered dying. She hadn't really made much sense of living yet, so having nothing to contrast, her perspective was about as mature as a mayfly's theories on evolution. The only thing that came back to her was the shimmer of the flying saucer with fluorescent lights, counting backwards by fives, a new skill she was eager to showcase, and then an inky vignette bordering her vision and swallowing her sight. The sepia glow from the edges of her view grew distant till the only thing visible was pinhole projection. She imagined this is what it must feel like to be a Loony Tune. They were always unwittingly falling through a hole in the ground, or running through a tunnel painted on a mountainside. *This must be the view from inside a mountain*, she thought. *I guess I'll wait for that pig to show up.*

Two things that looked like they could be the silhouettes of her parents. Two tiny dots, then more characters, soon the great drama of her life was filled with so many tiny little black heads that the light disappeared completely leaving a ring like an eclipse or a blinking eye. That eye had shed a single tear landing on her tongue. She could taste the sadness but there was no clue as to who it came from. All she knew was it was someone she hadn't met yet. She wished she could remember that thing Porky always said at the end of the episode. Having something to laugh at always made it easier to say goodbye.

Something about this sinking feeling felt heavy like sleep. When she came to, her parents had turned her hospital room into a temporary funeral home and preamble in memoriam. She saw framed pictures of herself nestled between every kind of bouquet available at your local supermarket, and some that she recognized from the personal collections of her mother's highest paying clients. She hadn't been out much longer than she was originally scheduled, but was still waking up too late to catch "Buffy the Vampire Slayer." She was even less thrilled than her parents finding out that she'd be staying the night in the hospital and missing the primetime block entirely. "What about our shows?!" She begged her mother.

"I know baby, but the doctors are still doing a couple tests." She explained. Eury was pretty convinced that Doctors didn't have to go to school anymore, so what business did they have taking tests? That must be why they have all of those framed pictures of cursives on their wall. At the time she was hoping that her dad would honor his promise to teach her cursive. Her first year at school had been rough on the whole family. She'd barely learned how to write her name, but she was hoping to start the next year ahead of the curve. She wasn't worried about it though, her dad had a talent for honoring special promises.

To Frank Carlson, Thrifty's ice cream was about as close to blind justice as Independence Day was to Lady America's left tit. He had a tradition to uphold. They had stopped for ice cream on the way back from every hospital visit no matter how brief. You could tell the emotional severity of the visit by the way he walked back to the car. That day they walked out of the chill of the Rite Aid hosting their favorite ice cream parlor and it to the heat with their cones stacked three scoops high and glistening with vibrant colors, a beacon bright enough to guide the sick, the poor, *and* the hungry to safe harbor.

She wished she could remember death. The first time that was, the second time was surreal but definitely going to stick out in her memory. But if she didn't remember being dead, then why was she so sure she was now? Out of the blackness above her head she heard a "bing bong" and could feel the chill of a well manicured pharmacy. She couldn't see anything, but carried by muscle memory she retraced the steps of her first resurrection. Getting closer to the Thrifty's counter she thought about which flavor she was going to choose and the word "vanilla" came to mind and began dripping from the ceiling.

She couldn't see it but clearly but she could feel the cold radiating from the display freezer and as she approached the floor felt soft like snow. The Snow drift grew till it was hard to walk through, eventually her legs became a nuisance, useless flesh and useless bones; vestigial. She left them in the hot sands hugging that corpse she left behind in that ditch. Without her legs she didn't need to take a seat, so she just floated up to and placed her hands on the counter. It was sticky like the cheeks of

properly spoiled babies. Her elbows kept sliding around without legs she couldn't feign proper posture. Her torso drifted up and Eury wondered if somewhere she was actually alive and comatosed, perhaps the doctors were expecting her to wake up any moment wiping the Cheer Up Charlie number right out of the first act. Maybe the Fizzy Lifting Drink she and Goose had consumed had reacted poorly with the drugs they needed to save her life or her heart finally gave out after thirteen years of relative wealth. Swimming down she found her legs packed in snow and gathered up clumps of snow and formed a ghostly tail. The makeshift oar would help her to glide around with much more efficiency, her upper body strengths was sufficient for gaining momentum but substituting her legs would help her navigate this spooky ice-cream parlor. The tail made of vanilla snow made her feel like a tadpole more than a ghost and with each passing second she grew more empathetic for the dead.

It continued to get colder. She struggled to move, the air was thick and rich. She rang the bell but its shape collapsed under her clammy hand. The cold distressed her so much she began to sweat more. She felt as if she was being frozen alive and burning up at the same time. The more she tried to get free the more she sweat, and when the sweat clung to the dry cold air her skin stuck to it like industrial strength glue. She was drenched in salivary panic and her body clung contorted in the air like a kid's tongue on a phone pole, or that same kid's missing poster nailed to that same pole a few weeks later.

This was a nightmare. She started kicking and screaming, but when she looked down her legs were missing. She was stuck floating in the air. As she flailed harder she ripped patches of her skin from the air, she was convinced she was going to die...again. Which didn't make sense, but the internal logic wasn't the strong suite of the fight or flight response. *This must be a dream, this feels like dream logic.* That was her speculative opinion, but she was guessing after all. *I guess I wasn't missing much,* she thought. *This was horrible. No this can't be a dream, because my skin really hurts and my skin's really gone; and if I move right now I'd become a walking figure from a medical textbook. Besides,* she thought, *this couldn't be a dream because--*

"Cup or Cone?" A voice called to her from behind the display case. She could see the corner of his triangular hat out the corner of her eye. The timber of her father's voice was unmistakable, only his habit was queer, but he had a smile that answered her question. She was dead and so was he, and now they would have the chance to say "goodbye" unlike the last time, and it was better than primetime.

DECEPTOR OF THE SEA

styled and photographed by
NICOLE MILLER
model: BRITTANY LAWRENCE

Sometimes I feel the incorrigible need

to get into hot water. I'll draw myself

a bath, raise the temperature by degree

the way you cook lobster,

plunge my ears beneath the surface

to listen to the water I'm making filthy

swish in dissonance with the ringing in my ears,

watch the steam rise from my face,

pretend I'm a bowl of lobster bisque

      (have I ever had lobster bisque?),

and that I've died my alleged

courageous death to be spared

the indignity of being eaten alive.

the pull

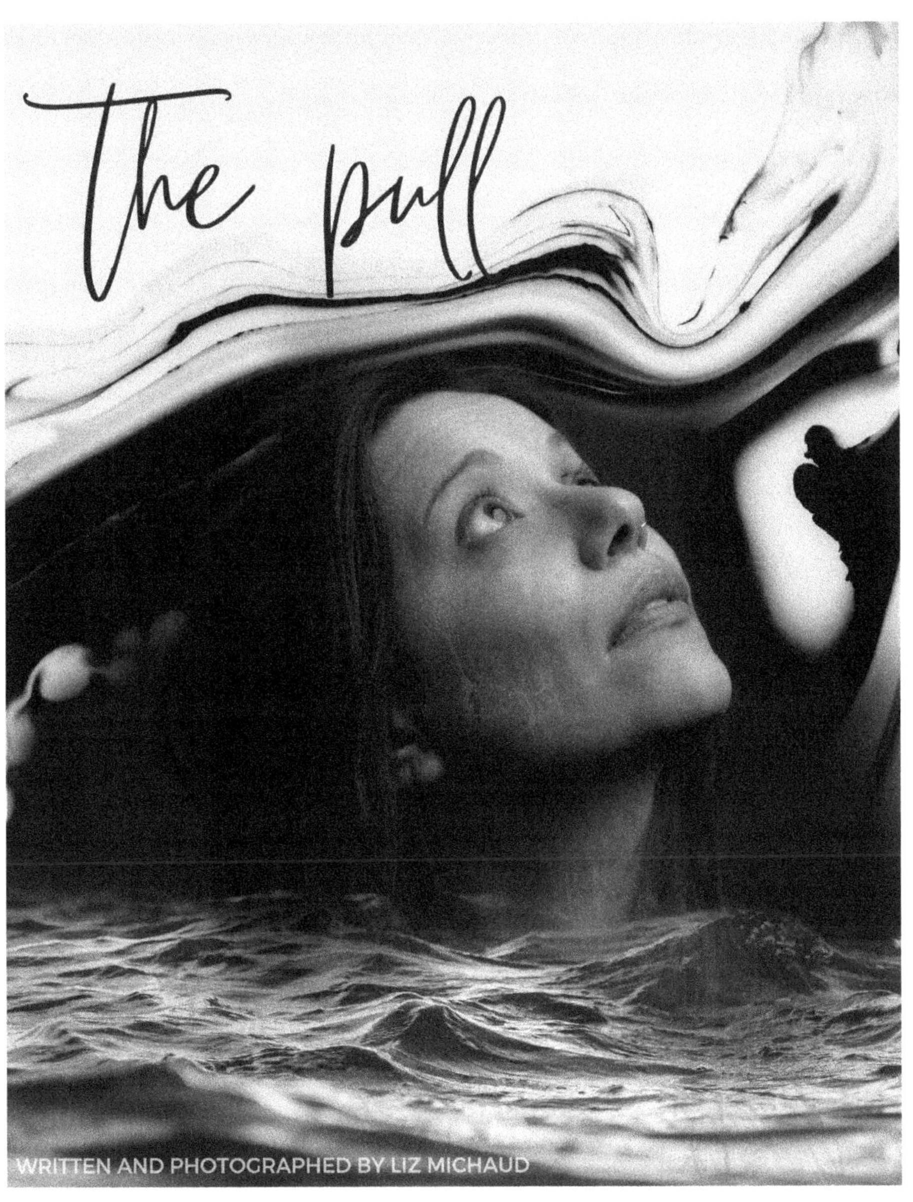

I hated this fucking house. I didn't want to be on this ugly rock. Not like you. You said you felt something close to magic here at Coal Beach, but there was nothing enchanting about the surly old fishermen in this coastal ghost town.

Dusty sun rays beamed in through the windows of your studio—so cheerful that I actually gasped and looked away. The sunset would have been stunning that night, but I couldn't bring myself to look. Instead, I shuffled through the kitchen, drew a bottle from the cabinet, and slumped onto the living room couch.

Darkness was already washing over this side of the world, details surrendering to the fog of night. Whisky smoldered down my throat as night swallowed the horizon, until everything was black except a steady pulse of light from some other house, on some other peninsula jutting out into the sea.

You'd been right about one thing: the place had a hell of a view.

~~~

I don't remember falling asleep, but I remember dreaming.

You're there, surrounded by swirling black ink, and just your face peers out of the murk.

Your mouth opens and shuts but only wisps of smoke pour out, your milky eyes focused on something behind my head that I can't turn to see.

I move towards you, asking where have you been?, and your face shrinks back into shadow. Reaching in after you, I grab hold of something wet and ropey, pull hard, and fall back as long strands of black hair unspool around me, coiling around my feet and up my legs until they swarm my torso and face and crawl into my open mouth—

When I woke I was already stumbling towards the toilet, the taste of whisky and bile at the back of my throat. I coughed into the bowl and thought I saw black tendrils of hair pooling down the drain as I flushed.

Some lingering nightmare residue. Nothing to be afraid of.

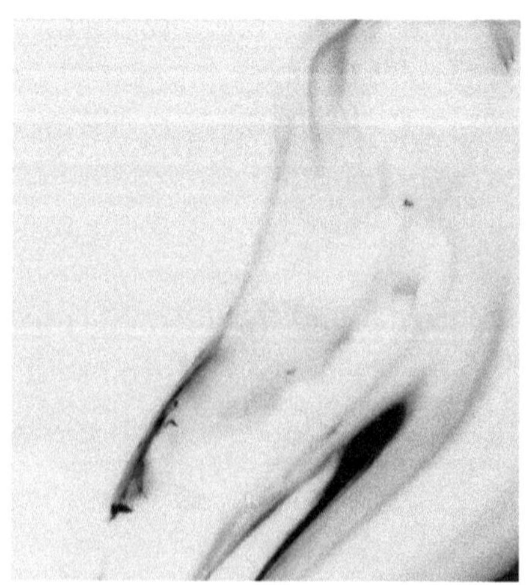
~~~

Detective Ornell found your body at dawn. Or rather, a fishing crew did. You were only ten miles away. He came by to make sure I would be okay alone here—whatever that meant—and that he had some follow up questions for me. "She was, ehm…" He cleared his throat and shifted uncomfortably "She was naked when we found her."

He continued, but a crackling noise building in the air all around me was clouding my focus. Sort of like…static electricity with the volume turned up. Ornell didn't seem to notice.

"You see," he was saying between glances and the floor, and his lap, and my eyes, "we found her gown, robe, and slippers folded neatly by the shoreline. Phone was right there on top—we told you that this mornin'" He glanced. I nodded.

"So we can assume that she was naked before she got into the water…" he trailed on, and I heard myself replying through the swirling clamour in my skull,

"Yes of course," I said, and "It's so unlike her."

More words. More glances. A longer pause. The whirlwind in my head roared.

"We also found signs of self-inflicted wounds." I could barely make out the words.

"That…" I answered through the din, "that's very unlike her."

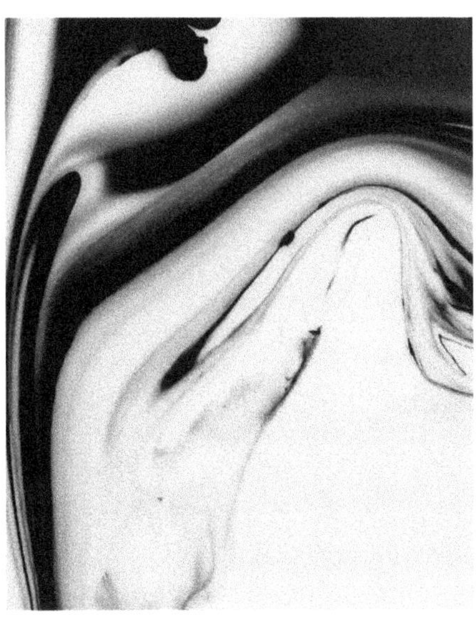

When we met we were both artists. But on the shores of Coal Beach there was only room for one. The careful balancing game of winning bread so we could make beautiful things tipped over when I collapsed at my show and was encouraged to take a "medical leave of absence." That's how we ended up on the island, living at Coal Beach. We should've painted the sign to say Burnout Bungalow.

You had insisted, My parents have an old cabin, perfectly vintage, and my series is already exploring Isolation.

Thanks to a decade of disturbing weather patterns, the island's only inhabitants were there to work, or had refused to leave their ancestral land. But it's perfect for us, you had assured, maybe there's room for two studios! It'll do you good to slow down in a sleepy town.

For the first few days we greeted every sunrise at the East window and gave evening salutations at the West. But soon, heavy grey clouds settled in and we learned that regular sunshine was rare here. Whatever spell the town had cast on you seemed to have worn off too; after the first few giddy months, you struggled more and more to paint. Your work became darker, more private. One time you caught me leafing curiously through your drying pieces—every canvas was layers and layers of black ink, running and pulling down the page in bloated splotches, yonic and vulgar—but you swatted me away, shrieking.

I began to avoid your studio, except to bring you tea, or food, or to ask if you were coming to bed. I'd usually find you staring out the window, doe eyed, and murmuring under your breath.

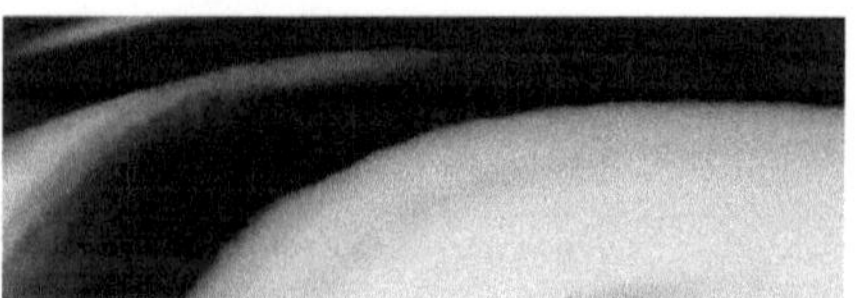

Six months after we arrived, your naked body was pulled out of the ocean.

~~~

Maybe this was the normal toll of grief, or maybe it was my relentless hangover, (or maybe it was because shadows twisted strangely in the corners of my eyes every time I shut them) but I couldn't sleep again that night. I lay face up in a bed that felt smaller without you. Like I could just roll to one side and slip off the edge of existence, falling into nothing forever, not even feeling wind on my face.

I must have finally drifted off as I watch the ceiling dissolve into an ashen sky. The mattress beneath me has also vanished and I am sunk up to my chest in sticky black mud.

There is a clattering to my left, and I can just turn my head enough to see a stone bridge leading out of the fetid swamp I'm trapped in, but I can't make out what's on the other side. It looks brighter over there though, and I can smell salty sea air.

The clamouring comes again and a figure emerges from under the bridge. It's you—I think
~~~

—but your body seems oddly out of shape. Too thin, too...nimble. You scuttle over the mud on all fours, gruesome and crablike, with a clattering net full of driftwood hoisted on your back.

You tear closer, panting and stinking of rot and mold, and I can only look on in dread. I cough and spit and wriggle as you stretch your net over me. Threads made from knotted human hair bite into my skin, and I know with a dawning horror that your flotsam trinkets aren't driftwood at all, but worn human bones. You heave me from the sludge an inch at a time, until finally I am unearthed, and you turn—still panting hoarsely—to haul me back towards the bridge. Towards the water. Towards the light.

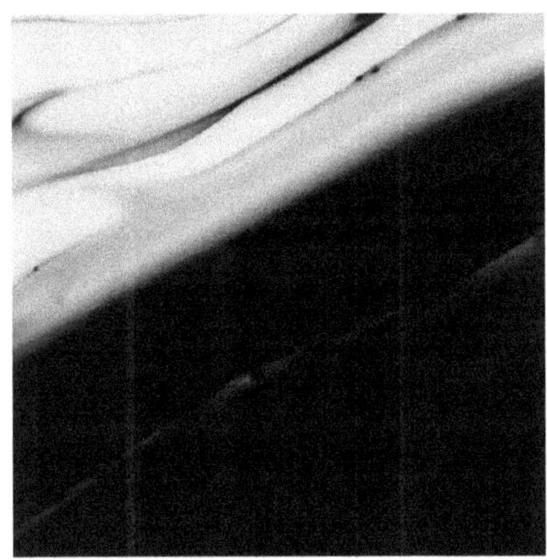

When I woke the next morning I wasn't in our bed.

I was standing in your studio, staring out the window into the morning haze. The fog would close in heavy and then stick around all day. I had seen plenty of mornings just like this.

I turned and stood facing your easel, where your last painting was still propped. I had scoured the shapes a thousand times when I thought you were just missing, hoping desperately for some kind of clue, finding only confused and abstracted pain.

Now though, as if a veil had slipped from my eyes, I could clearly see a body in the swirling shapes, struggling against darkness, peering out at freedom.

A shared nightmare.

My head snapped back to the window, where the mist hung heavy over calm waters; a smoke screen the colour of a corpse and as solid as a wall. At its center was a barely perceptible sheen, the muted luster of some ancient and forgotten star. The promise of dawn.

An unknown longing burned inside me. I might never know why you had gone. But maybe I could find where.

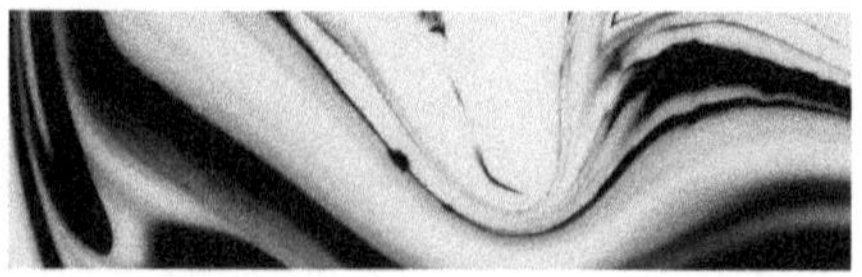

The mossy stones outside our door were slick with dew and cold against my bare feet. I carefully picked my way down our backyard and the crooked steps that were built into the cliff face a century ago.

Above me, I heard tires crunching up the driveway and slipped down the last few steps. I landed hard but ignored the pain of sharp stones underfoot and the sound of men's voices overhead. Car doors slammed as I unlashed the little rowboat anchored ashore and pushed it out into the water. The voices grew louder, and there was a loud rapping of fists on wood. Only a few paces in, and I was already up to my waist, my robe billowing in the water around me. I pulled myself into the bobbing vessel and looked back at Coal Beach.

Three uniformed officers stood at the cliff's edge. The fog curling in around them lit up with alternating red and blue. One of them, Detective Ornell, was already halfway down the steps, waving his arms. Crumbling stone had given out under him, and he couldn't get down any further.

I took up the oars and with one light pull, slipped backwards into the fog.

~~~

In the realm of grey and white, Ornell's hollering is snuffed out like a muffled radio station. Three more pulls of the paddles and I can't hear him at all. There are no rhythmic waves, no swooping gulls. Only my breath and the trickle of water rippling in my wake. My head is pounding with something like static again, and I hum to keep the panic and bile from rising in my throat.

I turn to peer behind me, into the white void, trying to make out any light, any visions.

Anything.

My tuneless song wobbles over the rippling water, bouncing into the fog. The paddles rise and fall, slow and silent, like I'm pushing through a viscous fluid. There is something else out here with me. I call out, "Hello, is it you?" and try to reach out with my thoughts. Where are you?

A quiet gurgling shatters the silence as water begins bubbling into my boat between two slats at my feet. I dart to stop the flow with my hand without thinking.
~~~

My heart plunges as I watch the oar I let go of slip from it's rung and into the dark water. I scramble to catch it, nearly upending myself, and more water slops in.

"No, no!" I shriek, clutching my remaining paddle and clamping down on the leak with my foot. My clothes, already drenched, cling heavily and slow my movements. My head swivels, looking for something, anything, out in the fog.

Looking for you.

"Help me," I wail, "Where are you? Why did I—Why did we come here?"

The boat fills quickly, the gurgling and bubbling overwhelming my makeshift plug. My foot slips and I fall back, smashing my head on a wooden crossbar, and collapsing into my boat.

"Please...Ornell! Officers! Please, I'm out—I need help!" I beg the sky, but if the wind hears me it doesn't answer. Water rises up around my cheeks and my head pounds mercilessly. The boat shudders as it descends, and the ocean roils beneath me, roused by my howls.

I sob and sink and thoughts that did not feel like my own fill my throbbing head. They snatched back her body, they say, but now yours will be ours, and ours will be yours, and we will all be we.

I'm screaming, or only thinking, I can't tell the difference anymore. And the voices in my head reply, there is nothing to be afraid of. There is nothing.

Finally, the little boat falls away and for a heartbeat I'm suspended in perfect equilibrium, until something tightens sharply around my waist and I am pulled, down, down, down, into the murky shadows.

And I become you. I am you and we are her, and them, and all of us.

And they swallow us all up.

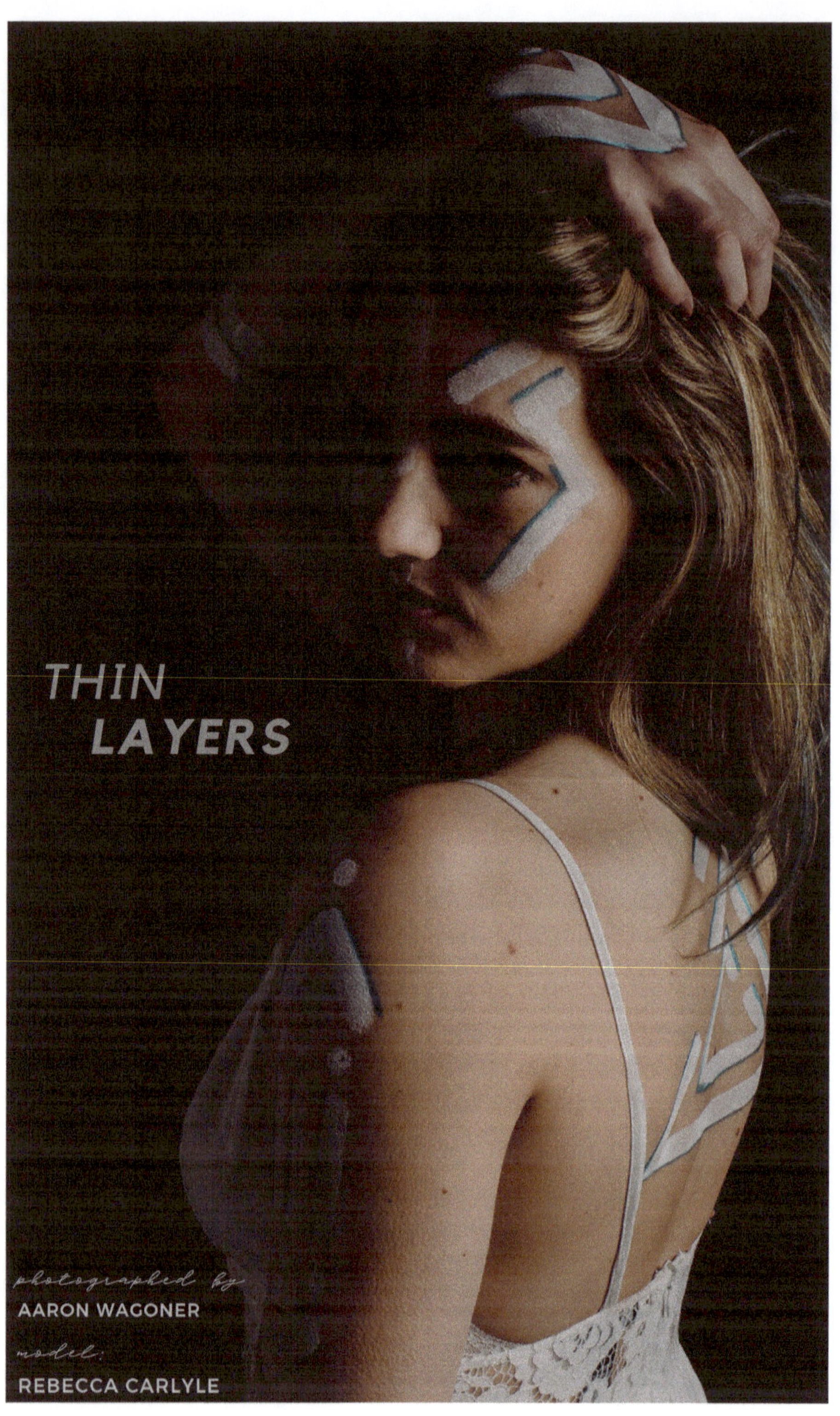

THIN
LAYERS

photographed by
AARON WAGONER
model:
REBECCA CARLYLE

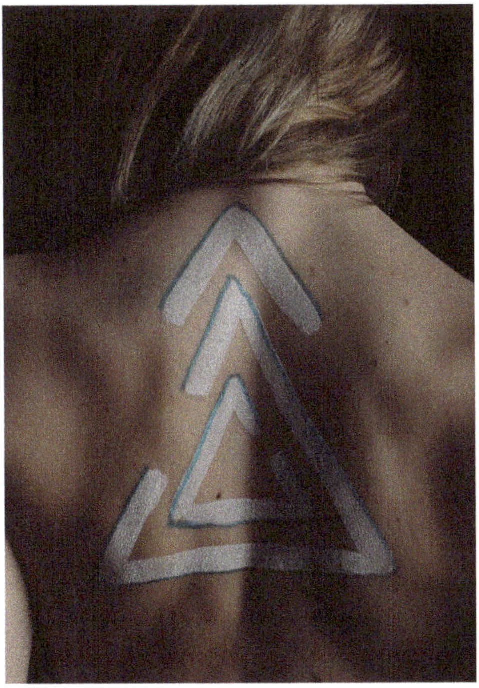

Celebrate your complexity—
there is power in
vulnerability.

Pisces Meets the Gemini

WRITTEN BY JORDAN NISHKIAN

You, my air,
you bury me—
hold me under,
carry me with you.

    When my knees betray my heavy bones,
    hold me, and I'll release into you like water,
    lapping and ebbing over you
    in towering waves.

I'll spill into you; filling
open spaces with currents.

    We meld, creating
    gorgeous chaos in our midst—
    mist becomes our blanket,
    and tidepools brim with life

seeking shelter from the crash—
fearsome, in the way
oceans erode
and rattle mountains.

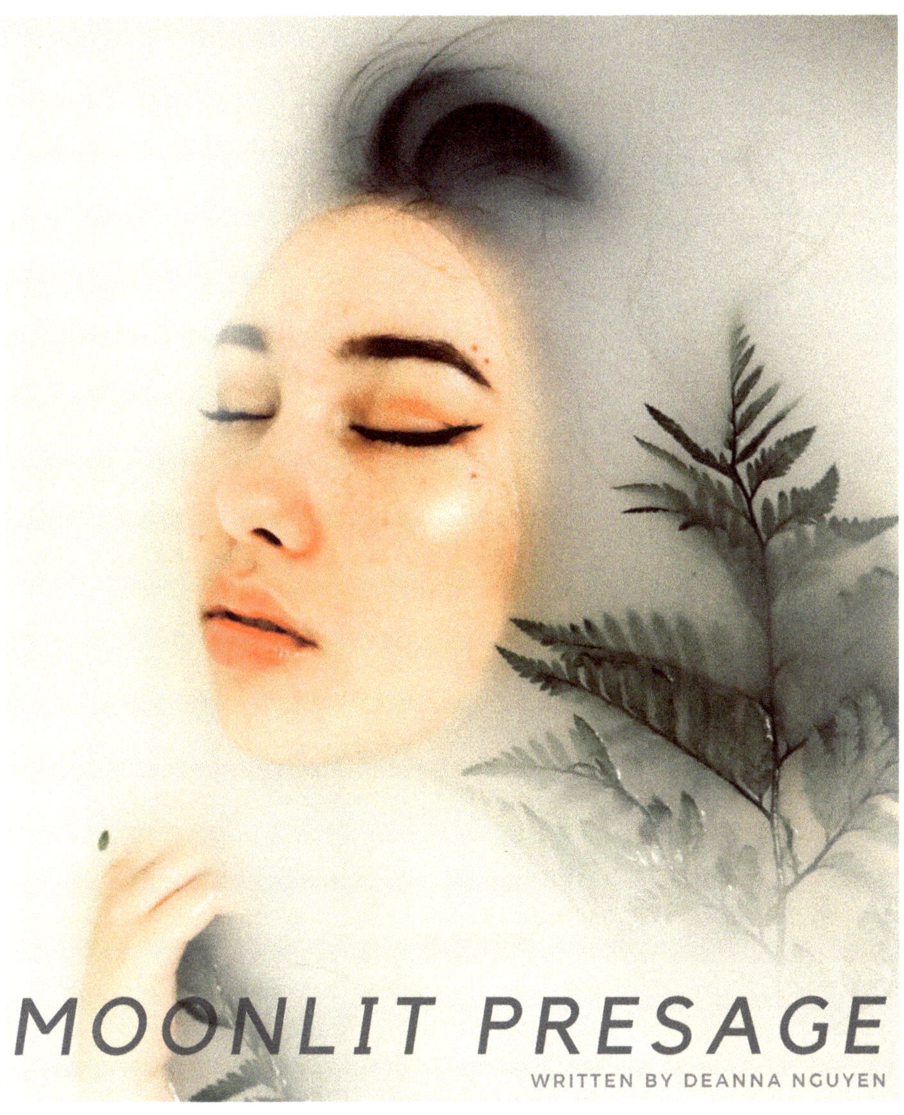

MOONLIT PRESAGE

WRITTEN BY DEANNA NGUYEN

A chime ripples the still night, unheard by those who dance in the garden of dreams. In a rowboat that weaves its way through Lunea's water canals, a hooded figure sits with a fox that's curled around her shoulders. The fox's vaporous form emits a white haze, her eyes golden and glowing. As their destination approaches, her ears prick up. The fox jumps off the young woman's shoulders, leaving smoky tracks that dissipate before she lands atop the bow. All the while, the bell's song resonates from around the fox's neck.

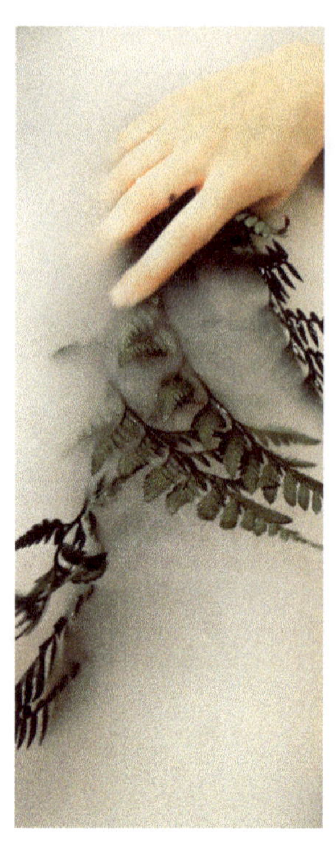

With no oarsman, the rowboat slows to a stop by the dock and does not require anchoring. A wiry man with stooped shoulders waves his hand as though afraid she might not see him, even though there is no one else around.

"Lady Naiya," he greets in haste, bowing. He clasps his hands together in prayer, eyes rimmed red. "Please, you must help her. She won't make it through the night."

Naiya steps onto the dock and Zuzu, the fox, jumps back on her shoulder. The man does not notice the creature. "Lead the way," she says as calm as the night allows her.

"Of course. This way." He gestures for her to follow him through the floating city.

As they cross an arched bridge, the man chatters. Naiya recognizes the nervousness in his voice clinching his words together. She learns his name, Aced, and that he has a daughter named Rya, who needs her help. A tingling sensation spreads out from the center of Naiya's gloved palms, itching through the silk.

They arrive at Aced's home where a candle flickers by the window. Aced opens the door and as soon as Naiya steps inside, dread cascades down on her. An uncanny coldness sweeps all around the house, encasing her in an uninviting chill.

Zuzu hops off her shoulder and pounces around the home in a flurry of bright light. The fox's cleansing ritual reduces the thick miasma but does not remove it. The chimes chase away the silence, a haunting melody that only Naiya hears. Once complete, Zuzu evaporates but regains her form moments later. Naiya closes her eyes and takes a deep breath, calling forth the moon's energy.

"Whenever you're ready," Aced says, his words tugging at hope and fear. "I will take you to her."

With a nod, Naiya trails behind Aced as he leads her to the bedroom. The miasma grows thicker, and when she walks in, she steadies herself against the wall. Startled, Aced moves to help but she holds up her hand.

He swallows and takes a step back. Naiya calls Zuzu, and the white vapors reappear, prancing around the room. She stands upright, but the weight on her chest does not grow any lighter. On the bed lies a girl who appears a few years younger than Naiya. Her breathing teeters on the edge of gasps and her body lurches upward every few seconds.

Aced flinches and chokes back a sob with a hand over his mouth. "My precious Rya. I can't bear to see her this way." He squeezes his eyes shut.

Naiya takes a step forward, watching Rya's convulsions. She grits her teeth when her palms grow more irritated. She furls and unfurls her fingers. "No one should see this." She turns to Aced. "I need to be alone with her."

Aced looks at his daughter, brow furrowed. He then nods and backs out of the room. "Of course. I leave her in your hands." With one last plea, he closes the wooden door.

Rya whimpers. The sound beckons Naiya toward the bed. On her knees, she examines the young girl's body. Pushing Rya's dress up, Naiya suppresses a gasp—dark purple blights fester and ooze black liquid all over her thin torso.

Rya's blights are the worst she has ever seen. Naiya's hands quiver before she clenches them. Shaking her head, she dispels her reverie. She peels off her gloves, revealing black veins branching out from the center of her palms. Woven through the veins are ugly, red ruptures. Closing her eyes, Naiya places her hands on Rya's torso, and instantly, the girl screams.

"It's okay," Naiya whispers. "Stay strong."

From the energy that she borrowed from the moon, Naiya's hands glow and, within seconds, the blights stop bleeding. In return, a sharp throb seizes Naiya's chest, disrupting her healing process. She sputters a cough, shielding Rya from the spray of blood with her arm.

Rya moans, her face scrunching up. Naiya resumes her healing, biting down her bottom lip to suppress her coughs. Her eyes remain closed, brow furrowed in concentration. She directs the energy onto the torso through her palms for as long as possible.

The blights shrink, but instead of disappearing, they transfer to Naiya's dark-stained hands. Once Rya's agony quiets, Naiya opens her eyes, gritting her teeth to keep her agony in. Her palms burn and convulse, the blights settling into her skin and forming new ruptures. She watches the black veins travel up her arms.

Rya's torso is bare and her face relaxes. Naiya pulls the girl's dress down and hunches forward, breathing hard. When she hears footsteps, she slips on her gloves and tightens the black cloak around her.

The door opens and at the sight of his daughter's peaceful slumber, Aced makes a small noise of relief and joy. Naiya moves out of the way so he can reunite with his daughter.

"Thank you, Lady Naiya," he says repeatedly. "You are our Savior." He stands up to bow.

Naiya tries to breathe as evenly as she can, but with every exhale, she nearly lets out a cry. "I must go."

Aced catches her tone and notices the blood on her mouth. He shifts his concern to Naiya and asks, "Is there any way I can help? How can I repay you?"

Naiya doesn't reply. She turns her back and leaves the bedroom. At the front door, she pauses. Zuzu returns on her shoulders and licks the tears that stream down her face. Naiya whispers, "Pray to the Tidemother."

When Naiya returns to the Temple of the Tidemother, she stumbles her way inside. Priestesses, each wearing white robes lined with silver, rush toward her. One kneels beside Naiya and wraps an arm around her. Another unclasps Naiya's cloak and strips it from her body. When they see how far the blights have traveled up Naiya's bare arms, they exchange looks of horror.

"Naiya," Nori, the priestess who holds her, says, "How many did you cleanse tonight?"

Zuzu licks Naiya's cheek before leaping down from her shoulders. The fox howls before vanishing—she doesn't reappear. Naiya swallows before answering, "Just one."

"You must summon her, Naiya," Nori urges. She lifts Naiya up with her legs and carries her in her arms. The other priestesses trail behind, murmuring their agreements.

Naiya winces from the pain in her chest and at Nori's insistence. "She won't help me. Not unless I return to her."

No one says anything as they head toward the bath house. As they enter, their hurried footsteps echo off the marble walls. The white, domed ceiling opens up to reveal the night sky. From the stone bench Nori lays her down on, Naiya sees the full moon and her presence soothes her.

"Quickly now," Nori says to the other priestesses as one begins to peel away Naiya's clothes. Two of them lift her into the steaming pool as the others scatter assorted flowers into the water. Naiya watches the roses, lavender, chamomile, rosemary needles, peonies, and lotuses float around her.

As the priestesses wash her, Nori studies Naiya's arms, tracing the tangle of black veins and red ruptures with her fingers. "The Tidemother is your only hope," she says, resolute.

Naiya doesn't meet Nori's gaze. "No."

"Naiya, you must—"

"My powers save people," Naiya says, her voice low. "I won't be of use if I'm with her."

"You won't be of use to anyone if you're dead," Nori counters, setting Naiya's arms back into the warm water. She heaves a sigh. "She calls for you."

At this, Naiya stills. She stares at Nori for a moment before tilting her head up to the ceiling where the moon gazes down at her. "'From the Tidemother we came. To her, we must return,'" she says quietly.

"Many of her children come and go but never stay around for as long as you have," Nori says. Her voice drops. "They fear her more than they fear death."

Naiya lifts up her arms and turns them from side to side. The corruption is evidence of the people she saved in the past year. She closes her eyes and remembers how their grief transformed into happiness. There's a power in that alone—one that Naiya doesn't want to give up.

"Please, Naiya," Nori says. "Summon the Tidemother."

When Naiya opens her eyes, she gives a slight nod.

Outside the Temple of the Tidemother, a stone pathway leads to a circular platform supported by a sea cliff. Naiya stands at the center in a loose white gown. Her tainted arms are a stark contrast to the chiffon fabric, appearing as though she's wearing long gloves. Nori and the other priestesses stand along the pathway, clasping their hands together in prayer. Zuzu still doesn't appear. The winds are not as energetic tonight, but the moon is a witness to what's to come.

Naiya doesn't need to clasp her hands in prayer or perform a dance ritual to summon the Tidemother. Instead, she waits. The ocean waves crash against the sea cliff from below. Before long, Naiya's skin tingles.

Naiya.

The waves subside and everything goes quiet. Unlike before, Naiya takes a deep breath and responds to the Tidemother's call. "Mother."

At once, the Tidemother's serpentine body bursts from the ocean's surface. Her gray-blue scales shimmer under the moonlight and her large fins spread out like wings. Her draconic head lowers to where Naiya stands. The mist emanating from the Tidemother envelops Naiya. She doesn't realize how familiar it feels—comforting even.

The Tidemother's icy blue eyes flicker to Naiya's dark arms. Her vertical slit pupil dilates. *You have spent too much time here, child.* Without letting Naiya respond, the Tidemother lifts her head. *It is time for you to come home.*

Naiya takes a step forward. "Mother, I—"

The Tidemother tilts her head back and emits a reverberating roar. *No child of mine will foolishly die just to save a few more humans. I will not stand for it.*

Naiya begins to clench her hands but winces, remembering the fresh wounds. She breathes in and out, keeping the fear that threatens to overcome her entire body at bay. "Please, I need more time. I promise to come home but I don't want my powers to go to waste." Naiya takes another step forward and holds out her arms. "No matter the pain, it doesn't outweigh the lives I've saved."

The Tidemother gazes at the moon. *That which you take must be returned.* She looks back at Naiya. *You wish to become the humans' Savior, but who will save you? There is only one choice, Naiya.*

Naiya can feel Nori's stare boring into her back. From the moment she agreed to summon the Tidemother, Naiya knew that she can't compromise with her. She has to at least try.

"I will go with you," Naiya says. "As long as you promise that I may return to the surface, with or without my powers."

The Tidemother doesn't say anything. She swivels around Naiya, cocooning her. *Your attachment to humans will be your downfall. For me to save you, your powers must return to her.* She nods toward the moon. *You will be powerless to save anyone.*

She meets the Tidemother's intimidating gaze. "This is my choice."

The Tidemother unfurls and holds herself upright. She glances at the priestesses before giving one last look at Naiya. Then she retreats back into the ocean and the waves pick up once again.

Welcome home, child.

Naiya walks forward and stands at the edge of the platform. She looks back and smiles at the priestesses. After bidding her silent goodbye, Naiya closes her eyes and falls forward, diving into the dark sea.

The priestesses rush to the edge of the platform and huddle around, waiting, in vain, for Naiya to resurface.

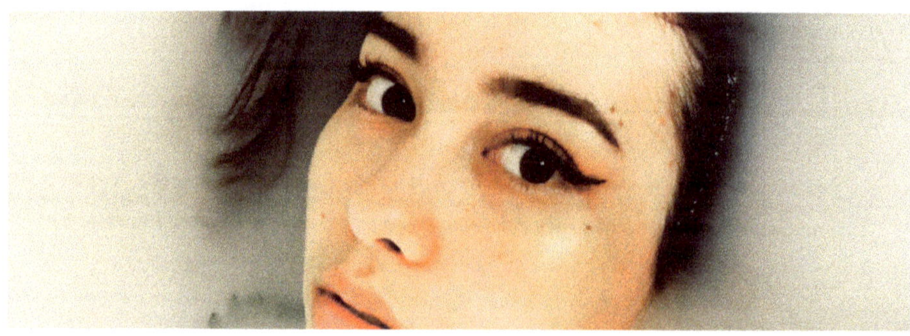

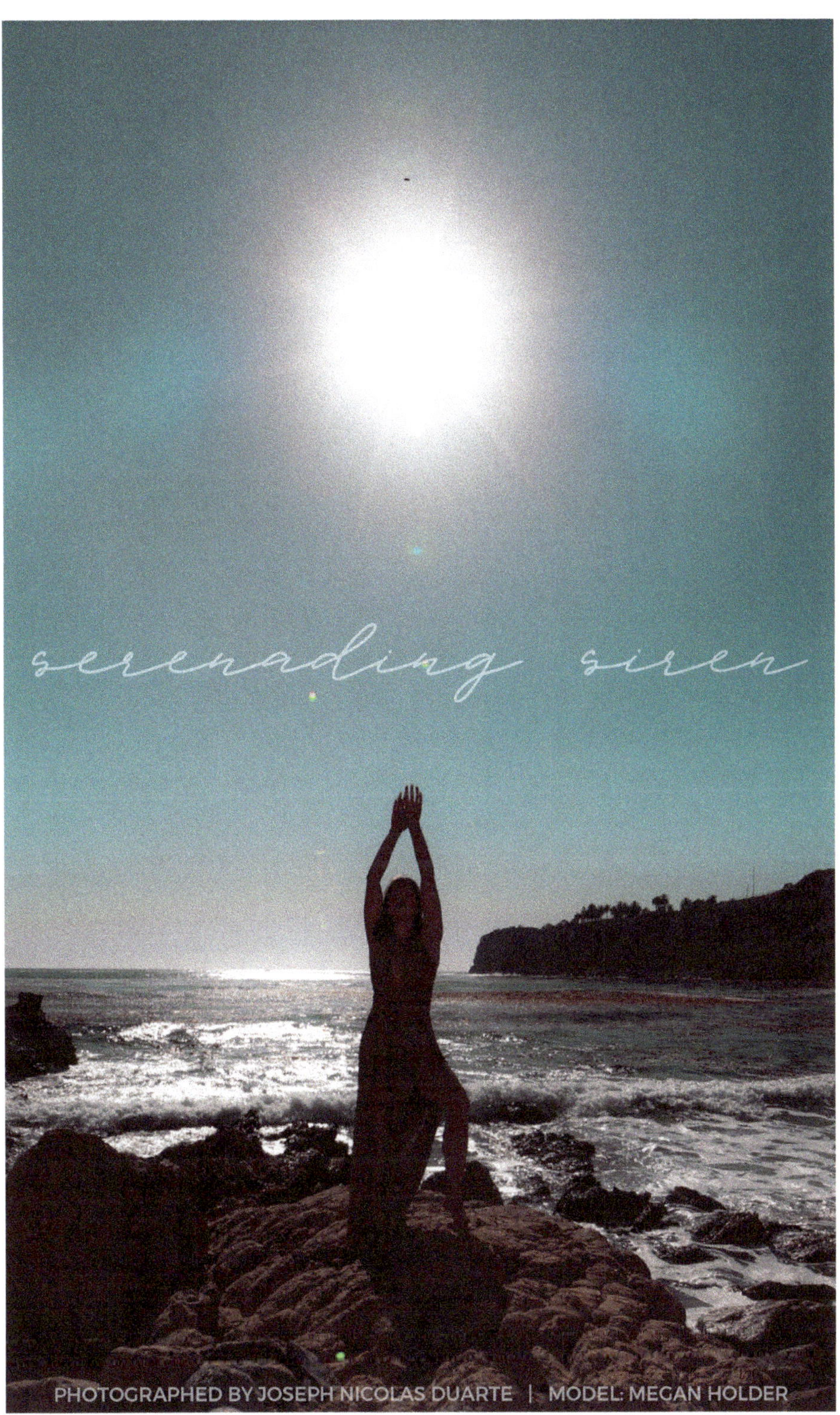
serenading siren
PHOTOGRAPHED BY JOSEPH NICOLAS DUARTE | MODEL: MEGAN HOLDER

She loves the serene brutality of the ocean, loves the electric power she felt with each breath of wet, briny air.

—Holly Black